# The Human Shore

# The Human Shore

## by Russell Thornton

**Harbour Publishing Co. Ltd.**
P.O. Box 219, Madeira Park, BC, V0N 2H0
www.harbourpublishing.com

Edited by Silas White
Cover artwork by Richard Tetrault ("Torso/Window,"acrylic/ board, 82 x 76 cm, 2001)
Printed and bound in Canada

Harbour Publishing acknowledges financial support from the Government of Canada through the Book Publishing Industry Development Program and the Canada Council for the Arts, and from the Province of British Columbia through the BC Arts Council and the Book Publishing Tax credit.

**Library and Archives Canada Cataloguing in Publication**

Thornton, Russell

    The human shore / Russell Thornton.

Poems.

ISBN 1-55017-385-5

    I. Title.

PS8589.H565H86 2006   C811'.54      C2006-903355-2

*All Human Forms identified even Tree Metal Earth & Stone*
—William Blake, *Jerusalem*

# Contents

# Acknowledgements

Thank you to the editors of the magazines where some of the poems in this book first appeared:
"Larissa Gypsies"—*The Antigonish Review*
"The Fire's Twin"; "The Ocean at Long Beach"—*The Fiddlehead*
"Summer Snow"—*Hammered Out*
"Blackberry Wine"—*The Malahat Review*
"Temple of Play"—*Prism*

Thank you to Allan Briesmaster for his comments on early versions of some of the poems here, and to Fiona Lam for her comments on a couple of the poems here.

Thank you to Silas White for his intelligence and imagination in his editing of this book. I'm extremely grateful for the benefit of his eye.

I

# Fifteenth and Lonsdale

Within the low heavens, I glimpse shadowy, rough garments
of cedar, hemlock and fir. Within the garments,
the mountain in its clinging-soil and deep-rock guise.
I turn and go when one light clicks red, and one light clicks green.
The two other people at these lights, who go in step,
pressed together in the damp cold, are each other's sweet pain.

I look up again—suddenly I know nothing except
that the mountain sits there secretly transparent as rain.
That it sees us. That it flirts with us. That it is a person
containing all the experience we can ever have.
That it is a pure signal. And whatever the two alongside me
are saying quietly to each other, they were made to say it.

The mountain sits, dressed in trees, and endlessly clear—
endlessly clear, and endlessly dressed in trees. It never ceases
turning our gazes back to us—it has no prophecy other than this.
The man who lays his blanket down on the sidewalk,
and spends the day nowhere but in the rain—I turn to him.
I remember again that I was born here, that in my life

I have gone to and fro along the hem of the mountain—
with the others at every corner, wearing my own garments
made of the trees. That we speak because the gods who travel
to the gods who remain need places to live. That the man mumbling,
asking for change, has always been a lover. The street mist
dribbles out of his pockets, becoming numberless names.

# The Ocean at Long Beach

*I need an ocean to teach me…*
            —Pablo Neruda, "The Sea"

The huge edge of the wind cuts away from me what I think I know.
That is how a man more myself than I can know
is visible in the surf—spray twisting to a lit screen,

a man like a brilliant diagram. Every moment, he steps out of hellfires
with the one he is rescuing his arm's length behind him—
his grief an ecstasy now as they arrive at blue air.

There they are within chaotic, unearthly rays. Then the wave's jolt,
its single pulse at its height, spuming thick white—
he turns to her, her hand losing hold of his hand, its fingers suddenly bleak

and reaching out of nothing into nothing, she vanishes. Every moment,
the wave shatters and is his abandonment and laceration,
it hurls and is his dispersal in the froth-lined, sliding tidewater.

I know I stand, living and named, in the place of my skeleton—
if I imagine the marrow within it I am touched awake
and I look out at a wave travelling to the far end of the ocean and back.

And what is not human turns, and is also human;
it turns, and as out of the throats of the presences, lets loose calls;
they echo in the wild driftwood, the wind-spiralled trees, the sky.

That is how a wave lifts and is a winding man and woman—
their dark way to and from each other is through the interior of the crest;
their chant fills and fills the skull of each waiting sandgrain.

The whole air here has a face. It is the face of an infant those two
break from as it is rises out of immeasurable sleep,
the ocean gazing out of it with its opening eyes; it is the face of the one

we hold in our arms when we hold each other, the one
we create and can never turn back and see—yet turn, as we have to,
to try to see, when it leaves us and becomes us looking.

# Foot of St. Georges Avenue

The boxcars couple, they shunt into the railyard,
their wheels cry all night, they play. The late work
at the dry dock beneath the hull-filled vault,
at the grain elevator, at the shipping terminal
with vessels lying up against the pier
and floodlit containers being shifted
by whirling, roaring cranes, at rail crossings
where I chewed car-spilled grain until my jaw
ached, and made rough gum—is play. No one sees
beyond what he sees when he runs, swings, screams,
no one knows more than a child knows. A boy
will look up, call for a father to put
a crashed electric locomotive back
on its perfect circle of rails. He will see no one,
and leave the room to look up the rest of his life.
The tracks laid down along the pale insides
of a man's arms gauge the same loneliness. The train
makes its pass the way his blood makes its pass.
In the festering he will focus on it,
in the hole he tears he will find it, the one
thing that is real, and any memory kill—
the slamming of boxcars into a vein. Now he can go
anywhere he wants in the night. The train
will take him, the switching will never stop. Below
the city block where my balcony hangs
and the avenue ends, the work keeps on. I don't know.
I don't know how it is that paradise is so wide,
the junction in the head so narrow. If you shut
your eyes, in the dark behind them you will
watch while eyes are rivetted into you.
If you listen to the coupling, crying, clanging
continue down through you, it will become a chant,
and that chant, what you know; then whatever you
are will be forsaken and finished. The sleep
you crave yet fear will come, the sounds and lights

die into what rises within you. A ferry
sits in fittings, a freighter rests, its deck loaded,
boxcars stand still, ready to be hooked up again.
What you dream, what transpires while you lie there,
is the beginning of the day you will wake to—
a world assembling itself, both workshop and toy,
a Christ entering metal, never to return.

# The Shaking Tent

*And yet there is only one great thing*
*To live and see the great day that dawns*
*And the light that fills the world*
(old Innu song)

On most days, you stagger together along gravel roads,
beginning at dusk, sniffing gas from garbage bags,
your jacket sleeves swinging loose at your sides,
hugging the bags close, your chins tucked tight
to your chests, drawing fumes up through your collars,
you armless ones, you go to shaking tents deep
in the bush outside town to sniff until dawn.

Give us, too, bags weighted with gas, show us
where to sit in the circle you make in the unheated
empty shack, let us learn to call all the spirits you call
into the tent, show us how to join you. Show us.
Give us bags to sniff from, show us how to do it,
there are so many of us, there are so few of you,
*and yet there is only one great thing.*

Until dawn, in the thirty-below dark,
while snow blows between our houses and dogs
search in their packs through the refuse and root
among yellow and brown stains where we have emptied
our honey pots in the snow, with our bags of gas
we will sit in the shaking tent, we will not sleep,
we will sniff and smirk and laugh crazily and cry.

You with your masters the caribou, the fox,
the wolverine who frees the world from any hold,
and the woman spirit, the fiercest shaker of the tent,
teach us to scream "I want to die! I want to die!" We will
make the sign of the cross—what can happen to us then?
In the morning we will walk out into sunlight
*to live and see the great day that dawns,*

we will walk out into the brilliant Canadian snow,
not to make snow angels but to shuffle toward home,
and on our way meet newspaper photographers
who ask us to pose for them while we laugh and push
each other aside to get into the frame and shriek,
"Take my picture, I sniff gas! Take my picture, I sniff gas!"
and later vomit and pass out alone in the snow—

to see the night, tents glowing beneath the moon and stars
like lanterns, firewood and pipe smoke, to hear
our grandmothers singing softly, to see the day
and sniff gas and freeze to our deaths in the snow,
in the shaking tents of our heads, in the cold, holy day,
for our mother the air, our father the air,
*and the light that fills the world.*

* *Kushapatshikan* ("the shaking tent") was an important
ritual among the Innu of Quebec and Labrador.

# Summer Snow

I sensed presences, looked out the kitchen window,
and saw dozens of Gypsies in the backyard,
sitting on blankets spread out on the grass—
all eating, talking, and looking in at me.
I went out on the verandah. Someone else
was there, a bearded man with an accent.
"Are they Gypsies?" he asked me. "Yes," I told him. "Roma. Gypsies."
"But many are White," he said. "Some have blue eyes."
"They're Gypsies," I said. "Believe me. I know."

The dream lit in itself a memory—
and I was out on a pier with a woman I loved.
I felt I had never been anywhere other than there.
"We're being watched," she said. "It might be best to leave."
I looked, and saw out on the nearby twin pier,
a woman standing straight-backed, radiant, alone.

On the return ride along that shore,
with the air arriving heat-laden from the Sahara
blowing through the rolled-down car windows,
we had turned to stare at an enormous
fiery orange sun sitting in the sea, half-filling the blackening sky.
It flared and glittered in the circular hollow
sweeping through the froth the waves lifted and spun to the sand.
We saw, suddenly, a large party of Gypsies
camped on the beach, sitting outside trailers,
gathered together in front of a TV set.

Then the dream relinquished the memory,
and I was again at the kitchen window—
where I now saw no people but new snow lying in the backyard,
though it was the middle of summer.
I looked up and saw no cold white flakes floating down
but transparent glass circlets falling, displaying
unfathomable radial intricacies, ever-opening centres,
and falling as if not from clouds but a sun.

Then the falling flakes that were not flakes
and the snow that lay on the ground had disappeared—
or had become invisible, what I sensed in front of me unseen.
I woke seeing myself waiting at a window,
knowing I had waited here before and would again,
and knowing it to be a halting-place, yet a place
where at every instant I was being informed
to gather up what I carried and depart.

# II

# The Fire's Twin

In orange glare, in smoke—the fire keeps growing, keeps approaching.
It shrieks at what it comes upon, it takes things up into a whipping brilliance—
though there are things it does not touch,
things it only hisses at and surges past. No one knows why.
It is as if the fire is searching, desperate
to know what it is searching for, desperate to see what is around it,
everywhere swinging its enormous smashed lantern.
It touches, it incinerates; and in that instant
it is as if it becomes a thing, and remembers—then the thing is gone
and the fire must keep searching, blind and lost;
the world is the elsewhere in the fire-gouged eyes of a doll.

Now over the charcoal of towns, of trestles—the fire hidden away somewhere—
the light that does not harm, that simply shines, that comes after,
the gentle light arrives. It, too, is searching.
It finds us, it takes up into itself much of what we are. Arrives
feeling the places the fire has been—smiling over the beds of ash.
And like the black hunger that swept through, it too is a command.
The ones who return to the homes they fled,
each of them is the fire's weeping twin, wrapped
in exquisite flesh, come to a mansion burnt
except for a threshold or a part of a door frame,
and must make up a song to be sung for a child.

# River Gravel

The mountains somehow shifting around each other
had been fooling me for hours. To try to think,
I sat down on a steep stretch of icy rock.
I saw a wind come off a sharp peak above me
and agitate a darkening mist. I stood up
and began to run. I slipped, slipped again, crashed
face-first with my legs wrenched into natural trap-holes
where the months' snow lay over treetops
until, after two hours, I reached the snow line.

Then I was in forest, on quick-changing ground
difficult to see. I kept running, kept crossing
and recrossing deafening creeks, trying to find
the right river origin, the right way back,
and kept marching down creeksides through bush
that cut at me, belittling me, goading me—
until finally I understood, until I began to feel gratified
at how more and more of what I had thought
to be myself was being stripped from me.

The way ahead was the same surging black space
I carried within, and was all I was, and I could go
nowhere but to the centre of that space
and to the presence of the man who had fathered me.
I spoke to him. I told him how I had been a darkness
to myself for years as I had run, the way echoing
my every question with no sound—only a blank wall
of matter and will. Time had happened. It had filled me
over and over with my boyhood without him.

I saw ahead a turn in a creek where it joined
another creek. Red markings on a high boulder
signalled the beginning of a river that would lead me
out of backcountry and into a familiar valley.
Slowly I waded waist-deep into the swerving melted ice
to get to a bank I saw I could make my way along—
but out in the middle of the flow lost my balance,
grabbed at water, sensed it take hold of me, propel me
for an instant, then blindly I found the riverbed.

When I righted myself I had a fistful of gravel
in my hand. I released it, watched it pour out of my palm.
The river, always gathering itself up as it rushed
through the touch of pure distance to the inlet,
had let me stand and gather up my father.
Wet and shining with the last light, the gravel was a mirror
in which I saw how my face was my father's
with gravel falling out of his eyes, how the crushed stone
was the river in its bliss grinding mountains down to tears.

# Nadine

Night of quick, wild rain, gusts off the inlet. Blackness
lit only by glintings of rain, bored through to nothing
by my car headlights. I stood waiting on the pier.
She stepped out of the blackness and into dim sheen
and faced me, saying nothing yet gesturing. At first,
I thought that she couldn't speak English. Then her friend
was there beside her, down from an unseeable ship.
The three of us piled into my taxi. I apologized
for not realizing that she couldn't speak or hear.
The two of them in the back seat, the friend giggled,
chattered half to himself, while she sat forward and leaned
toward me, and I saw how even in her widest smile
she was wound back inside her to where
her own trapped screaming deafened her. But here
she had her hand on my shoulder, touching at me
to turn, turn left, turn, turn right—knowing I knew the way,
and at every instant teasing, flirting. Then the laughter
in her eye-flash in the rear-view mirror undid me,
the clamped-down face with which I peddled myself
trip by trip fell away. We were together, the three of us,
the wind at the black glass around us the breath
of a childlike presence welcoming us further, further,
the rain on the roof metal the tapping of a heart. They taught me
how to sign *no problem, friend* and *asshole.*
They were Similkameen, they were my age,
and had been in Vancouver a month. They had gotten
an American twenty-dollar bill for the taxi fare
from the ship to their hotel and back again. They gave me
all of it, refusing the change, the money adding up
to more than a decent tip. The friend, the girl's cousin,
her sarcastic, playful, hilarious pimp, told me
the sailors had made fun of her, and neither of them
stood for that. Anyhow, the sailors sent her back. Get us
*somebody else,* they said. *We want a talking whore.*

# Wharf

The tide in, the water swaying deep and slow—
a man will know the sea is the sea, nothing else, and yet know a gull
spiralling down, shrieking through the raincloud-roofed sky,
arrives here and takes up the sea in its beak.
A bow of twine gathered from four turning, infinite distances,
it lifts away with a magnificent present.

The gull will vanish, the inlet reappear—
and a man perches alone at the end of a platform. All he understands
how to mouth, all he must forget so he might go out from himself
in the gull's shrieking, will return to him,
scavenged bits of the cold beauty of the water in it,
the inlet swaying a moment in every word he knows.

The man will stand there, intact,
he will protect what he is. He will go out again and again from his wharf,
lightly in the world and a part of it, and bring with him
what he sees of what he is not in the water's glittering, in its heavy dark—
he will go out circling wider and wider
through the waiting aperture of himself.

# Rain City

*It was I who covered the earth like a mist. My dwelling-place was in high*
*heaven; my throne was in a pillar of cloud. Alone I made a circuit of the sky*
*and traversed the depths of the abyss.*
  —*Wisdom of Ben-Sira*, 24: 3-5


The rain thickening its static. The hissings, whisperings, outcries—
sounds the inside of a radio is searching through. The rainclouds
come in off the ocean, halt at the mountains, slide down through forest
and down along the rivers and creeks, across the inlet,
and the rain-mist winds in through the city streets, the back alleys,
to swirl around the dumpsters, crows, seagulls, sparrows,
around the people who sleep outside, and around the one
whose shawl is the searching rain-mist's glow, whose veins search—
and who is a rain-eyed bride, and goes about the city,

the alcoves and curbsides, to meet an invisible wave,
to open herself to it, take it into her, let it fill and warm her,
and feel it pulse and undulate through her and feel it is the one true song.
There are the sounds the half-block-away high-rise suites
keep within walls of rain-blurred glass—the sounds of desirers
who try to find themselves in each other, who hear their names
and bring to a culmination the trial they conduct unknowingly
in the court of their searching carbon, where their names
are the same as those who buy her, as those who seize her.

There are the sounds of the despair no grief can enter. That go out
in the crow's cawing, the seagull's shrieking, the sparrow's chirping,
and become wilder while the mist presses closer, blinder
at the alleys' entrances. The machines on the city's wharves hum louder,
the inlet ships' horns groan louder, and the rain turns colder.
There are the sounds of the clipped cries of those who can do
nothing except search for the ones gone missing from the alleys,
while the rain-mist floats through like the smoke of burning sweetgrass,
while the fallen raindrops circle and lock themselves in pools,

while the rain pours down into the city harder. There are the sounds
of a funnelling alley wind—and of vessels smashing, sparks scattering.
There is the rustling, the stirring of wing-feathers, the quick flowing,
of the alley dove lost in its dark Jerusalem of rain, and the sounds
of this one calling softly. There are the struck and bruised ones,
and there is the rain-mist that hides in their veins and the sound of its voice:
I am nothing but a path. Your body is the way you look for me,
and the way I look for you. Your body is the way you look for your body,
and the way the rain-mist moves through the song-wet streets.

# A Worm in a Wild Apple

The white flowers flutter, float down and lie in grass
like fine drops of sweat in the crease of a woman's back.

The leaves fall, the apples fall or stay, vanish into soil or air.
Once I saw a tree that had collapsed in the night—

its branches riotous, laden, straining its roots and trunk,
the tree knelt to the ground. It bowed its head, and laid the crown

of its branches in the kingdom of a field full of apples.
So the limbless one, the brown-ringed bather in the earth,

the eyeless seer, discovered and tunnelled through the soft fruit,
came out with the sweetness in him of what he had gorged on,

and like a nameless son of the beginning and the end,
lolled in the apple flesh on a luxuriant couch.

If a man could become drunk enough, eat enough of sin,
know enough of parting, and become nothing but a blind god's path,

the ever conquering love he could only fail to imagine
would take him into itself, and he would fall and fall

the way of the tracings of the love's turning and turning—
under the worm's sun, moon and stars, he would ride the blossoms.

# III

# Larissa Gypsies

In the out-of-the-way taverna I come to every day,
a Gypsy family is eating an afternoon meal together,
the moustached father not looking up from his beans and bread,
the trio of shoeless children, all girls, preening themselves,
the young, worn mother looking away intently yet unfixedly.
Two passersby, other Gypsy women, stop,
turn their heads and launch an insult across the handful of tables.
The young mother launches back an apparently inspired response
and instantly the exchange escalates into a full-blown verbal brawl.
The women outside begin shouting, spitting and making obscene gestures.
The woman inside begins shouting, spitting and making obscene gestures.
The taverna customers, the dozen or so of them, keep quiet,
until after some minutes a young man sniggers uneasily,
then another slips a glance at the taverna owner.
Suddenly, the taverna owner, fed up, marches to the Gypsies' table
and orders, *Get out! Get out! Don't ever come back!*
The woman, however, is not paying him the least bit of attention.
Her husband, expressionless, is still calmly eating,
her children are calmly putting the last of their food into their mouths.
Now the taverna owner tries to forcibly remove the woman from her chair.
*All right, all right,* she ends up relenting, *We're going, we're going,*
and finally stands up and walks out, husband and children in tow.
And now most of the taverna customers have stopped eating
and become an audience for the afternoon spectacle.
The taverna owner is out on the sidewalk shooing the Gypsies away
while the three Gypsy women continue arguing, dancing around each other
and uttering forth a concoction of Greek, Turkish and Romany.
Even the Greeks, who have known Gypsy people all their lives, are awestruck.
These women, awkward and uncouth at the world's table—
they are the unbroken ones, never to be corralled,
fierce, free, and playful out there in the air glistening as with their own gazes,
they are like winds from a wildly loved nowhere, laden with savage roses,
they are like scattered living tarot in the street.

# Larissa New Year's

If you were lucky, you said, by the end of the night
we would have the money for a holiday
on Evia or Alonissos, on Thassos
or Halkidiki—or we could even go to Crete.
All New Year's Eve you beat men at cards—
one by one they exited the game.

I sat back at the bar and watched
and thought of the night we had met,
when you stated you foresaw deaths
then tried to forget—the neighbour, the relative,
the stray kitten you introduced to a mother
and her brood that hissed it away.

And you told me you were a thief. I admitted
I, too, had stolen things—for a time—
but now to find metaphors was to pocket
new money. I wanted to steal a thing
from its class and marry it to an alien other.
You nodded at that—all contradiction,

calculating, vicious in an instant,
yet frightened and soft-hearted
in a way you had to hide. People either died on you
or deserted you. But I had no choice—
I had to stay to see the constant startled look
in your green eyes, to see you perform

your ritual behind a half-closed kitchen door
with olive oil and floating flame
to keep away the evil eye, to see you dab
holy water on your throat in crazily driven taxis,
to see how you stood as at an interface
where gods and goddesses appeared.

Nicotine addict, gambler, who thieved
everywhere, who also gave without thinking,
you foresaw nothing of the thief
who came for you yourself. Or did you?
Every holiday you took, you might have half-meant
to lose him in a lit street. That startled look,

you sensing he had begun his work in you—
the way you somehow knew what cards
were in players' hands. What I knew was the cutting
of the New Year's Day cake going wrong,
the coin wrapped in waxed paper not to be had
by you or me that year—and then, not any year.

# A Woman and Child

Sharp-eyed, in multi-coloured skirt
and high heels, with her free hand
she holds out roses and takes coins,
with the other, clutches and breast-feeds
her linen-swathed infant.

The instant collapses, and the clear
morning sunlight is a dream
of the foetus in the womb—
the watery mystery knitting
a lightning of flesh and bone—

now of the milk of eternity
suddenly flowing freely
over tables, into stalls, alcoves,
through clothing racks set up
along the aisles of the bazaar.

She draws her blouse, turns,
quick, musical speech on her lips,
and the world flashes, her earlobe's bangle.
Every word I have learned
goes after her, clinging to her neck.

# The Summer Grass

Evening sunlight and just-cut lawn—

a lamb shorn for the first time,
and slapped back into the field
as its wool is added to other wool and taken away.
It feels the air now as never before
on its naked hide, shivering, and uttering a hoarse cry.

My grandfather at ninety, his hair
still thick and wavy, getting his last haircut,
about to be gathered up unaware.
(*Got to get a haircut. Haven't had a haircut
in a long time*, he would keep saying,
when he'd had one that morning or the day before.)

I see him seated in the care facility's hair salon
with elderly women getting their perms,
at any second about to turn to the stylist to ask,
*What the hell am I doing here anyway?*—
an innocent, wrinkly lamb, with human eyes.

He disappears into the green radiance,
the strange pain of happiness in the summer grass.

# My Grandmother and the Cherry Tree

The backyard tree's mass of pink blossoms
fully arriving that moment, filling the sky around her head,
she sits down out on the verandah to light a before-dinner cigarette,
and begins talking and gesturing and laughing.

She is never tired, she says, never the least bit.
It is so nice to be here, just think.
But tomorrow, being here will only be a memory.
The weather has changed so suddenly.
It is so warm, she could have worn a sun dress.

The weather has changed so suddenly—
as if time has sped up and the late spring might turn to summer
before I drive her back to her room at the Lodge.
The summer might turn to fall before she sits, a large bib
snapped onto her, at her next dinner.

I might come to visit her, and have to look for her,
and realize I have not recognized her,
white-haired among the white-haired with walkers and wheelchairs.
I might stand off at a distance, unable to move,
and see how frail and see-through she has become,
yet see how she is of the same darkness and heaviness
sitting in the mountain outside the window.

She cannot see the cherry tree, she says.
She tries but she cannot see it.
But we know, we know she is blind now.
We will help her stand, lead her inside, sit her down,
then cut her food for her so she can eat with us.

The tree's loose blossoms float down to touch her.
It cannot see her. It cannot try to see her—
though if it could try, it would look out through every last blossom.

So all this evening, the tree can never be tired,
and is wearing the delicate pink dress of a girl
who has a shining face and smiles and laughs easily,
and dances the Charleston late into the night in the Roaring Twenties,
a cigarette in her hand, the burning ash never falling.

# IV

# A Peruvian Knife

Tooled in the leather of the hilt
the outline of a condor in flight.
Old tribes tell how ancestors
sacrificed virgins to a bird—
the women's spirits would join
the invisible army of the sun god.

A love gift. Light and slender
like the one who gave it to me,
and numerous-layered, the steel
alloy and softer, darker metals
melted and folded onto each other
to form a pure and single whole—

like her and how she is folded in
upon a love burning beyond
the passing fire of any parting,
where all that can ever happen
has happened, even death. Her centre
is that seething bird's twin,

the pulse through muscle and bone
the hammer and tongs, its own
bladesmith lifting from it living
unseen weaponry, annealing
then tempering the curved
edge to the tip in the blood—

the talon of light that lets it
pierce into the world, the world
made of lovers who are killed
while they dream, lawless, wanting
to be forged into a blade of law,
to die in order to escape it.

# The Frog Pyramid

Up where the sunlight falls
on the pyramid top, was where
they who climbed rough steps
or were borne along ramps
stood and performed rituals.
Little else is remembered
of the significance of the place—
only that the costumed priests
congregated here to worship
the frog as a holy animal
for its fertility, for its intimacy
with rain in a rainless land.

But the shape of this mass
of piled-high mud bricks
is that of a frog, and the shape
of a frog, that of a set of four
vaginas arranged together—
and I imagine priests who lived
to ascend the warm sides
of this altar to conjure and rule
the potency they could know
as creatures of standing mud,
and see by a world of water
and earth through water and earth.

At the base of the pyramid,
near a main winding path,
unmarked, the whole altar's
presiding hundreds-of-years-old
human remains. I look down
at what is lying uncovered
in the earth-box of the grave,
a half-mummified female,
decapitated, the head in place
at the end of the neck. Weights
of darkness in the air now,
the lustrous adolescent eyes.

Here is the woman who lies
always within the engorged
phallus, with the head severed
to free the flow forever. And turning
in his desired terror to kill,
as he gazed into her face
the priest must have felt terror fill
with what was almost love. Then this
was lost in the blinding draw
of the terror opening him wide,
and all was nothing but the price
of his way to the god in the light.

*Huaca Pucllana ("sacred place of playing"), Lima*

# Temple of Play

A small hairless dog
with upreared orange forehead hair. Of a breed whose origin is lost.
Whole head a visor, haggard
human-seeming eyes, tongue
hanging out the side of its mouth. It is also a tiny deer.
And a corner of shadow
in the cornerless glare.

*

They worshipped death.
Their severe-faced descendants, when they laugh, laugh smoothly
and hear the dry barking
out of Jesus's wounds; the clattering note
on the holy mother's lips.
They walk in single file to the priest,
and they are offered dust.

*

The dog solitary—
the light-gaited wanderer of the site's grey earth. I see it everywhere
off to the side of the kohl
outlining the eyes of the woman leading me. While death
shines in her slender white calves. While death
sits layered and angled
within the piled mud bricks of the altar.

*

Here they swung a barrier open
for a living person only once. The close sun touching completely
the breasts of one obedient and astonished,
breasts tipped in death.
The elaborate intent in what they did—
she knows little of it. And yet
her own walking by is a knife.

*

The dog squats near me,
sallow-haunched, still,
excrement falling out of its anus. It looks at nothing but the sun.
Its eyes are the vast
transparent eye of the dust, the eye
that hides within my skeleton. It looks out
at itself in whichever direction I go.


*

Here they prepared food, they ate,
then broke, scattered and buried
underfoot all the bowls and plates. Now one of them turns to me,
black-edged, exquisite in the expanse of light—
though it is she who brought me to this place
and who kneels in front of a cross.
What can my bones do but lie in dust.


*

Her glance, her smile,
they make death happy. Death lets the dog's eye display its jewel.
It allows my eyes to leave me, and in the dust
making and remaking us,
I find us. As if from there,
that distance away, where my bones grow bright,
I glimpse myself dancing.

*Huaca Pucllana ("sacred place of playing"), Lima*

47

# A Circle of Bones

As you go ahead of me, yellow steeples silhouetted above you,
through a plaza with its pigeons and little children selling crafts,
through intricate-carved cedar doors, arched hallways,
past walls of holy paintings, reliefs of saints, each covered in gold leaf,
through a courtyard filled with brilliant slow light,
and into the ornate colonial cathedral, I follow,
and as you go down below all this, into half-dark,
small and slender, half-turning to me in quietness and knowing
out of the straight-falling bright black of your hair, I follow.

I go down an enclosed narrow stairway of rough stone,
into a tunnel, crouching but hitting my head, drawing blood—
the air the breath in the mouth of the dry sand and stone—
and I follow farther through the turn of a second tunnel, a third,
until we reach a storage-way, a foot ledge along a wall,
to the side of us large open wooden boxes that hold stacked human bones,
and after this, open vaults in the earth that hold piled human skulls.
I follow still farther, down more steps, through a final tunnel
until we walk out into the deepest and largest chamber.

In front of us is a white core, a cluster of about a dozen skulls.
Around the core, as if issuing out in every direction,
are leg bones laid side by side touching at the joint ends,
white rays emanating out to a circular band, two skulls thick—
then an extension, an expansion, a second set of bones, twice as numerous,
then a second ring of skulls, the completion of a corona.
You explain to me that it was all arranged in this way
by a discoverer of the catacombs, and kept this way
with an enclosure built around, and no one can say why.

The mass graves those who would lie in them were told to dig,
the dirt crypts into which the human corpses were bulldozed
tumbling over and under one another like adult rag dolls
but with skeletons sticking out of the starved bodies, dead eyes staring—
images of these come piercing into me, then disappear.
This half-lit cemetery beneath a church, this collection of bone
centuries ago divested of flesh, the flesh vanished into a now-scentless air—
if uncovered and re-excavated with expert care, how is it
it was re-ordered into a radiating sphere if not out of spontaneous love?

It is like a Tibetan monk's container of essences—
that art performed by the devoted and meticulous, that weeks-long work
placing coloured particles of sand on a design set on a platform,
completed only to be erased, only to be deliberately swept away,
and every particle of sand poured into a river or stream.
Except, in the hard, solid substance, in the colour no colour at all,
of its host of skeletal pieces, it is known
as nothing else is in the play between us and what sweeps us away,
and made to stay, and made of what has stayed of forgotten ones.

All these hundreds of eyeholes that flashed in the light
when they held living eyes, when they opened into the blackness of pupils,
have been taken up in an eye radiating in the direction of the sun
that once shone on the skulls' flesh—and is still burning in this eye,
in its each carbon cell, like an awakening one seeing nothing but the first light.
And as you go ahead of me, and as I come around alongside you—
we stand gazing with eyes that are our only maps, and are the maps
of this eye that has been waiting for us and will gather us in,
and show itself to us as us, this bone sun, this circle of bones.

*Church of San Francisco catacombs, Lima*

# The Suspect

The four of us stood with our backs to a bright wall.
One stared straight down at the floor, one sneered
to his side, one kept nodding off, starting to fall
then righting himself again. Only I wanted her to see me,
to know I had turned away from another and was floundering
out into the night when the ghost car swerved to the curb
behind me and I was brought here to a row of men
hung with numerals black and precise as weapons.

I wanted to be the chosen one, the one announced
as winner of a TV game show's grand prize,
the one selected for a classroom's highest honour.
I wanted to be recognized, clearly identified,
and magnified in the midst of the versions of men.
I could feel her standing there a few feet away
from the lineup room, behind the wide dark pane
and looking in, the pure, the broken, mystery.

I wanted her to point to me and answer her questioners,
*Yes, he's the one who did this to me.* I wanted
to be caught in just this way, then taken to where
I could wait alone, knowing I would see her again
in a court of law, see her face to face at last.
I wanted her to say under oath, *It's him.* I wanted
to be able to watch her from the witness stand
while I was being questioned, and confess, Y*es, I did it.*

I wanted us both to lie perfectly like this
so I could then be sentenced, incarcerated, the two of us
connected for life. We would feel the exquisite one
gaze out through our faces at itself through steel bars,
through walls of thick glass, across guarded tables
while we touched hands and repeated old words
worn down by time, no power, no knowledge flowing
through any others deeper or more indifferent.

# V

# Basement Room

Carrying cinder blocks I stole from building sites
mornings before school, I would circle the house sealing openings. At night
I would shove a door across cement, bring a plank down across it into a slot,
and barricade the basement against the bush out back, the others upstairs.

I would turn from the door and see huge rats shaggy with brown fur
drag themselves away, and I would dart deeper into the dark and shut
myself in my room. I had read how rats could gnaw
through half-inch-thick steel and how ship rats lived inside

cow carcasses kept frozen in the hold, reproducing every five weeks—
in the time of one voyage they mutated into things that could stand cold.
But I lay there where I would be nosed through by the rat's snout,

where the inside of my skull would be scraped by the rat's teeth,
so when a window brightened again I could wake suited to fear and hate,
and watch my concentrated love run and hide in the corners of the day.

# A Wave

Now I remember what I dreamt. The wave came to its crest
and was a brilliant animal rearing up
at a barrier, blasting my ears with its roar.

The living froth poured vision. The lit spray contrived a crown.
It halted, swivelled, and in vacant agony
stood tearing itself out of its own time-deep bowels.

It collapsed—a flung and shattered clay jar;
innumerable lost seashells flying, spiralling whitenesses
around what melody they could. Then the snarl

and the thud of the whole bulk hitting the shingle gulley.
It slung up the beach a foam of running marrow, whispering.
And now the bed, desk and chair hold their notes,

while the small clock ticks to calm a wildly lonely child.
The itinerant particles of dust, lying sparkling on the floor,
seal in what makes the child cry out and the darkness smile.

# Blackberry Wine

The moon in octagonal windows, twin portholes,
passing silver over her half-the-couch-long hair.

All evening, she bottled wine, now she sleeps,
her face a figure's on a prow. It must be that in her dreaming

the house is a sailing vessel filled with the scent
of blackberries. The ship lifts anchor, the tide is with it,

the wine of her is beginning to flow—and she is leading
the ship, giving it life, she is brewing the wine.

The cache of ripe berries is stirred and crushed
in boiling water, the mixture strained and stored,

the juice poured into bottles and fine cloth fastened
over the glass mouths, and the juice collapses its structure—

all as she sails out into endless scent and transparent
purple-black gloom. And it must be that in her dreaming

she has searched for and found the ship's lost helmsman.
If she awoke now, she would find her hair wine-damp,

and find the one she allowed to stand within her
was one within whom she herself had always stood—

the two of them out under the full sail of the invisible,
in the moment of the wine steering through the wine.

# Concerto

Somewhere I was listening. Sleep had laid me down
and fixed me on a waiting slab. I saw you across the room,
a heavy-curtained wall behind you. You stood
at the tips of yourself, a trembling lit haze. You were
as I knew you, but less yourself than a child gazing out
through its own widening questioning. I felt
what flowed from you begin to rush over me: music,
relentless, searching. Music, and surgical instruments
that cut into me, bringing pain indistinguishable from joy.

I felt the flowing go out from myself as well as you—
watched you disappear at the other end of the two-way
current into deepening brightness. I sensed a hand
touch me on the shoulder. You, the one I had faced
in the sunlit day, had come into the room
from another room where you had been playing a piano—
yet it seemed I could still hear the sounds of the chords
and notes lifting off the keys, interlacing themselves
into the melody, perfect, inevitable, unknown to me.

It seemed you must still be at the piano, something
of you still escaping from within the music to come to find
what it was in me that was listening. You were again
at the curtain. I turned suddenly—being delivered
into my own waking hearing and seeing as into air flowing away
over a fresh grave with the music, with what I had dreamt of you.
You stood close to me, touched me on the shoulder,
and I shouted—the one note I knew, all I knew. Just now able
to hear how loud, with you leaning over me—I shouted.

# Window Curtains Half-drawn

In the upstairs room, the half-drawn
window curtains swell and flutter and flare.
Here she sat at a table and sang to herself,
spreading out a square of fine white canvas.

Measured, cut and folded it, made flawless
elegant stitches in it. Hung it and it began
to glow as if a temple dancer turned
within the drifting folds—bringing forth

the dancer and bringing forth the man
torn apart, scattered and collected up
while in the dancer's embrace.
In the upstairs room, in the full sunlight,

I follow the turnings of the singing
and the contours of slowly dancing air
out across rooftops and high tree branches.
It is how I come to stand in a stone street

beneath a window at which a woman
waits, subtly leaning. I follow the way
through the black glass of that hair,
the charcoal and pearl of that shoulder.

How I feel the pulse in the flesh I wear
travelling from the invisible to the invisible.
Yet how, from where I stand in the room,
the quick ray in the curtains, the small gust

and swaying, is a breathful of syllables,
the name of the one who lives in the house.
How the syllables are a sewing
of what I see to what I cannot see.

# Raccoons

Suddenly raccoons were treading the yard: three
came delicately to the patio, to the sliding glass door, and halted—
and for an instant peered into the front room, their three
soft flames flaring through all my cells, blinding me. I knew I had

heard them say something, but did not know what. They were there
only to not be there—except for the dark, the brightness—
and that way, as much as any animal existed anywhere,
they presented proof of what could not be made into lies,

they brought out into the open what was circling within my sight,
treading within it to more than my sight. They will always be
disappearing into a thick hedge, leaving the sunlight

like a transparent empty screen, exiting at the far edge of a story
that has hypnotized me. I come to, and the tellers are gone,
but I feel warmed, lined with a fire that does not burn.

# Mudslide

Too full of the force of the rain,
the creek is letting out a sound
of a thing that cannot be soothed.
The trees snap. The water-weighted,
steep hillside abandons itself—
its earth separates from earth
like a freight train derailing.
A man and woman's house is thrust
off its foundation—the two
are buried in debris and mud.

If we take arms against troubles,
or are laid down from the first,
we cannot help but lose the names
of all we ever do. He said,
when the slide hit, it was as if
he lifted out of his body
and was nowhere. She was thought lost
to the river ramping below,
then found where death had found her
beneath the pieces of her house.

We say goodbye to what we know
of ourselves when grief enters us.
We discover the way back
when love becomes our truest grief.
We will come back—will come back
to other people. And will say
a name we know for a person
when we refer to a hillside,
a creek, a river, and a rain
that fell and does not stop falling.

*North Vancouver, January, 2005*

59

# VI

# The Function of the Purest Grass

*at each moment sorrow grows in the world,*
*it grows thirty minutes per second, step by step,*
*and the nature of sorrow is double sorrow,*
*and the condition of martyrdom, carnivorous, voracious,*
*is sorrow, double sorrow,*
*and the function of the purest grass, double*
*sorrow*
*and the joy of living we suffer from doubly.*
        —Cesar Vallejo, "The Nine Monsters"

The function of the purest grass
is to wait for a wind to rake it, for the sun to explore it
and kill it, for summer wildfires to use it
as a path and leave little of the path behind,
to wait, to tremble, patient and forlorn, for thunder
to fold down into it and clouds to roll rain down each blade.

The sad singer, the murderer, the lover
who is the bright eradicating one—they pass like grass.
The shiver, the loss, the comfort moving deep
through the flesh, the trespass that opens its abyss—
transpire like the wavings of grass.
And the war beginning, and the war over,

and the dance of uncanny joy through the streets—
happen while sorrow grows like grass.
Grows more and more pure and more and more vast.
And remains—it flies free, returns, remains. And might remain,
the prayer inside prayers, though everything
we know, including grass, is gone.

# The Sleep of Water

Where it is all crushed to whiteness
the quick creek is statuary marble,
the powerful hearts of wakefulness
that flash within the marble flash
from the other side of water for us,
and beat and press against dazzled air.

The shapes they know in the flowing, here
concentrated in the down-rush, here
leaping in the boulder-edged spate,
are a charging horse and chariot
that halt and immediately fall into slow-
turning pools, calm glidings along clay—

then they become the face of one
full of the peace at the furious height of love,
whose eyelids quiver and go half-closed
like those in the lineaments of a Buddha,
then the face of a child who speaks
and is immediately asleep, dreaming.

And in the bright day, that is the face
of the sun in the thousand-windowed
church of the creek, the overflowing
treasure chest of a wave, the crystal
drift of rain, a bird's flight, the face
of petals so blue we lose words.

And in our dreams, that is the child
awake in dreams lifting open eyes to us—
though water will find its level, and we
will never descend to it and stay
the selves we recognize, we will never
begin to feel enough sorrow or joy.

Water flows to us and away, whiteness
in the interior rolling flames of our bones—
we want to touch the transparent cheek
in the water before it disappears deeper
into us, kiss this child without parents
whose countenance is no one's, is our own.

# The Unfamiliar Name

*Love is the unfamiliar Name...*
—T.S. Eliot, "Little Gidding"

I
The trees turn slightly, some with full early leaves,
some with new needles like green tears,

they turn and sway slightly, dripping with rain
they turn their polished glass, the sparrows whistle-sing

while sunlight finds its way through clouds
to glitter in the trees, the air sways slightly;

the sun lets itself break into countless pieces
outside the window of the single room

of the basement suite surrounded by trees
on the morning after the night we have lain here

as if we have been instructed to do so,
as if others have come close and guided us,

have taken us by the hand down into this room
so they can arrive and we can know them—

the resemblances, the ones who are all we have lost,
the first ones, those from whom we have come;

they arrive and urge us, they crowd softly
in my eyelids that lower as in sleep or death.

## II

An inner door that has always stood half open,
and a woman behind it, light falling to her

through a secluded leaf-touched upper pane—
the light arrives, brightens, is one of the others,

naked and leaning at an ancient washbasin,
combing out her hair, coming to lie down

and becoming you again, now light
lying down in the room and at once lost and found;

there is a tightrope of illuminated strands
twisting and flowing between us, stretched out

through the air under a circus tent;
there is a taut music moving in the tightrope,

time humming and whispering, time singing
while it burns along the tightrope marrow;

we look out around us into the room
out of a single opening wound

that searches through us, a question we do not know;
our lips are a small child's against a dark window.

III

They undress us of our names—the one, the kohl
of the other's eyes, bringing light into his eyes,

come to teach a labourer and a king his name;
even if what we make is for the dark,

even if what we do is the last thing we do
before the wave hits, before the bombs fall,

those others, able to do nothing but love,
those hidden ones who always dance with time,

they can only wind through us, only shatter us;
like a woman whose hands have their own life,

shaping a jar from wet clay, working with pestles,
the look in her eyes the look of the first woman,

you conjure a woman within the plenitude,
within the now-filled hollow you hold before us,

you lift your face to me, it is not yours,
it is all the others', you gather me up

in your eyes, you show me the others' eyes,
and finally each of us falls away.

IV
What imagines us, what in each of us
searches for the other, what lets us know

we are mirrors, are images in a mirror
we cannot see, we follow to meet our blindness—

light softly answering light or a hawk
sinking hooked feet into a tiny bird;

we follow, we wear out as if dying,
we gather up ourselves and gather up glass,

of which we were the silver, and the rain
into which the sun gazes, lost and searching,

gazing at itself in its brokenness, leads us,
and we are reached through as glass is reached through,

and we come back, and an unfamiliar name
is swaying in us, clothed in us, clothed in mirrors—

the sun continues searching, finding and searching,
the trees turn slightly, some with full early leaves,

some with new needles like green tears,
they turn and sway slightly, the sparrows whistle-sing.

# Seashell

They said that it would let you hear the sea—
that it echoed the rushing of your blood.

You listened, you sensed no sea, no pulse reach your ear—
with your family around you, you took in the sound

and had your baptism, a plunging in air
and the vanishing of anyone who might have named you.

And this bright, brittle husk you find now
while walking out along an empty shore—

you hold it up to the sun, you look at it until
your eyes forget you, until they go free, and go

ahead of you and bring you in among coilings and spirallings,
the way of a self-fabling, self-estranging cry.

# Story

You may have been waiting—as you knew now you had always
    been waiting—
in the dark gathering within you, in the slit of light opening
    within you.

You may have seen a sky go softly cold, white manna lying
    in the boughs of the fir,
the entire backyard lifting, wavering and parting before you,

the way out of Egypt opening in sudden radiance,
the flaunting flood in the chest just as soon about to close the way.

And you may have gone, you may have departed into the pure promise
    of the unknown,
but what you could say of where you had gone when you came back,

or what you could say of your life—your loving, not loving, being loved,
    not being loved,
and the miracle of the panic—was that you were standing, staring,

that you were hearing a bird cry, you were seeing the bright blade
    of a wing,
that there was a seagull flying close and low through falling snow.

Russell Thornton was born in North Vancouver, where he now lives, and is the author of several collections of poetry. His most recent book, *House Built of Rain* (Harbour, 2003), was a finalist for the Dorothy Livesay Poetry Prize (BC Book Prizes) and for a ReLit Award.